ESSENTIAL MUSIC THEORY FOR KIDS & BEGINNERS:
(FUN ACTIVITY WORKBOOK COLORING BOOK)

SERIES: BOOK #1

This book contains 33 tailor made music pages created by an experienced music professional and teacher whose goal is to bring the best results for the beginner through an interactive experience.
This book is book #1, part of a series of books on music and focuses on the treble clef.
It's a workbook as well as a coloring book, on big 8.5" x 11" size paper.
Other books by Livingcolors Publishing and Avery Fisherman
will cover bass clef and scales, all important and essential for a budding musician to
learn to keep on progressing. Made ideally for kids ages around 3-10 & beginners, this book is designed to
help teachers and parents really hone in on the fundamentals and basics of music for their students.
The information covered in this book is vital to know for all instrumentalists including singers.
The contents have been made so that it's easy and fun where the beginner
will enjoy learning about music while coloring and writing and drawing.

Coloring can also help improve focus, improve motor skills, have fun, relax, reduce stress,
reduce anxiety, improve self-expression, stimulate creativity, learn about structure,
improve spatial awareness, improve self-esteem, and more.

Copyright ©2022 Livingcolors Publishing & Avery Fisherman. All Rights Reserved.
This book is copyright protected. The contents of this book may not be copied,
reproduced, redistributed, duplicated, or transmitted in any manner whatsoever
without direct written permission from the author or the publisher except for the
use of brief quotations in a book review.

ISBN-13: 9798428459401

Just For You!

A FREE GIFT TO OUR READERS

Additional coloring book pages from some of our favorite books! Go online to

livingcolorspublishing.com

MUSIC STAFF

0

1 & 2 & 3 & 4 &
WHOLE NOTE

1 & 2 & 3 &

DOTTED

HALF

NOTE

1 & 2 &

HALF
NOTE

1 & 2
DOTTED QUARTER NOTE

1 &

QUARTER NOTE

EIGHTH NOTE

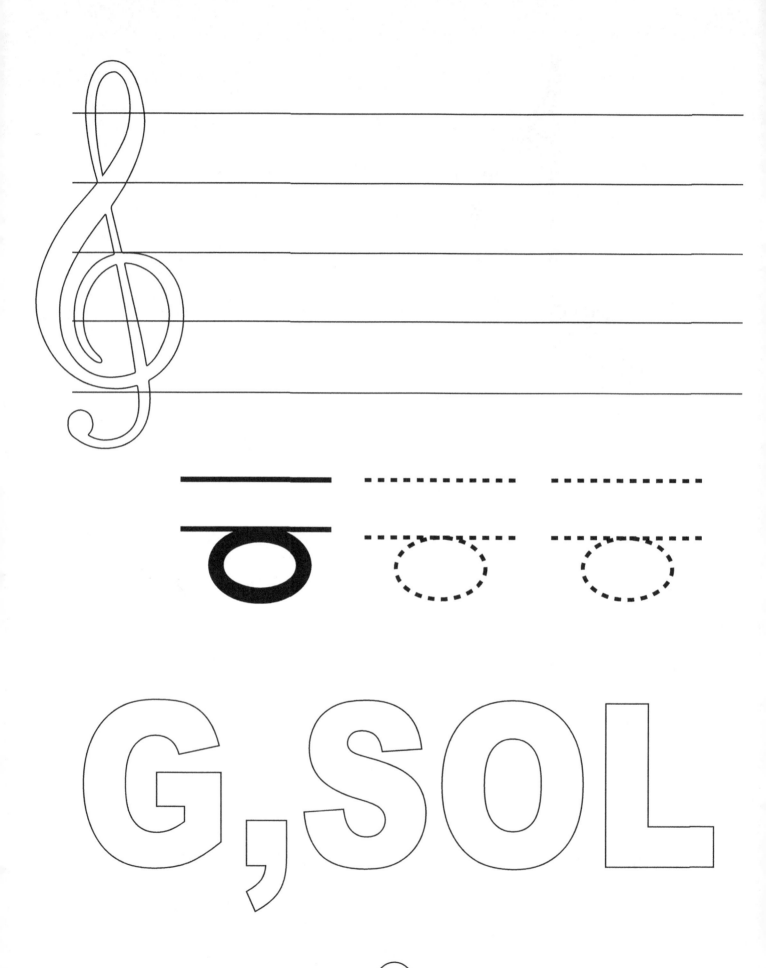

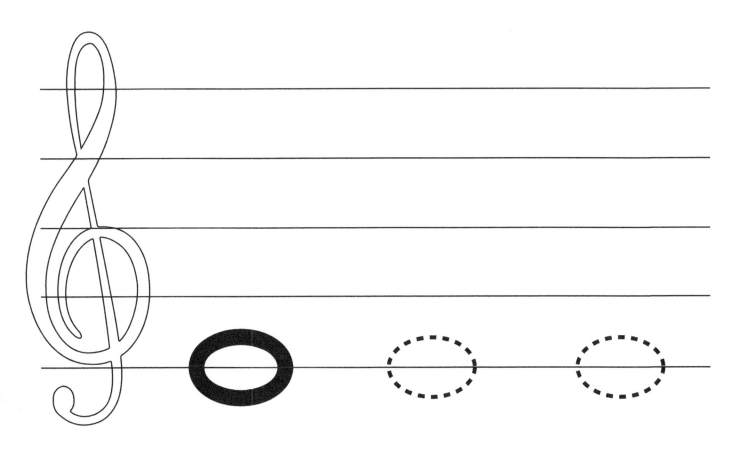

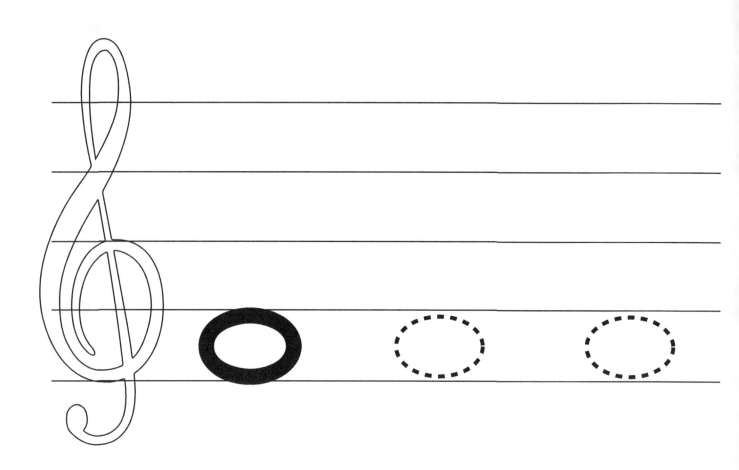

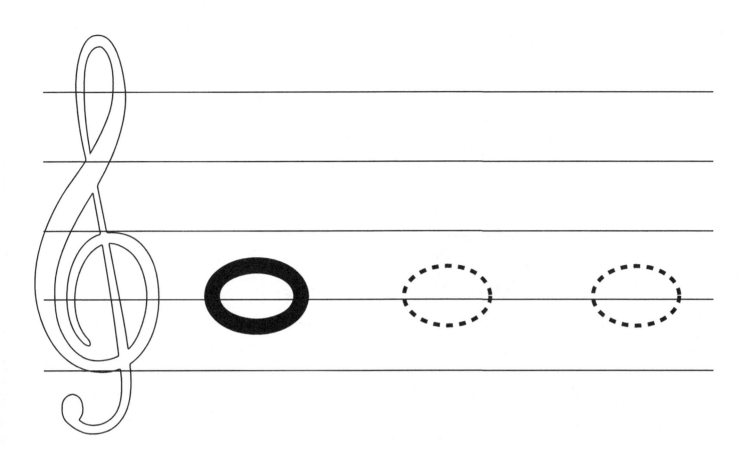

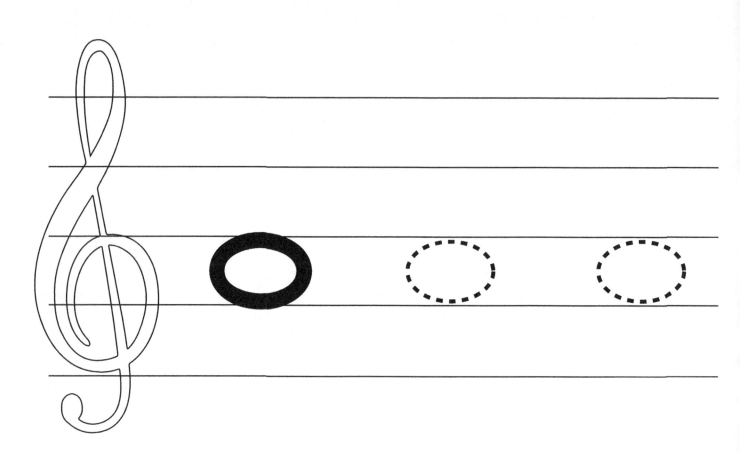

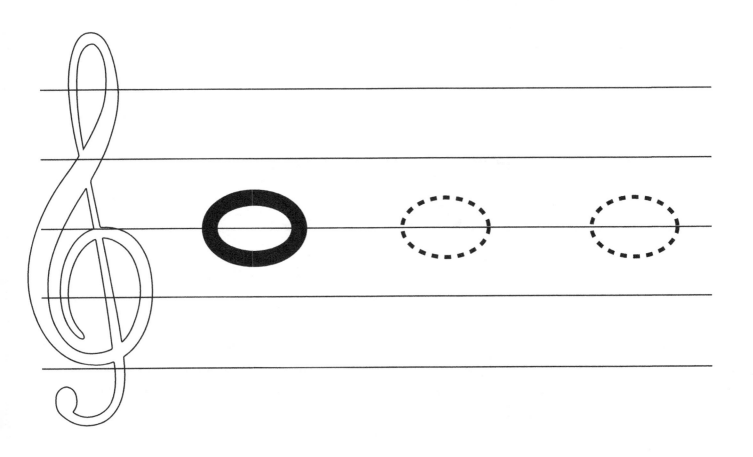

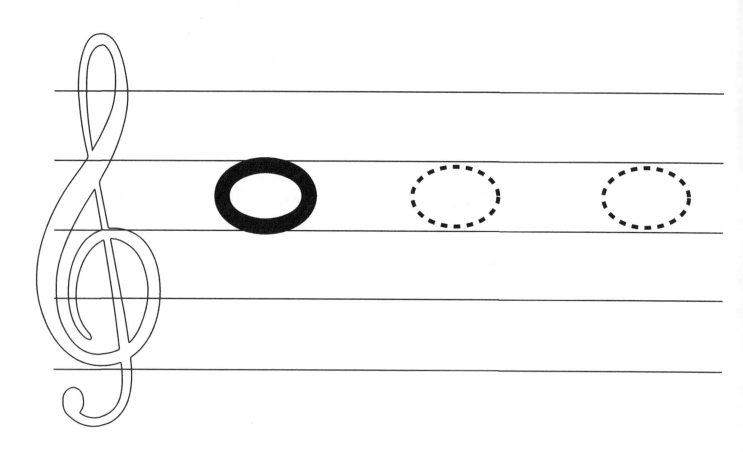

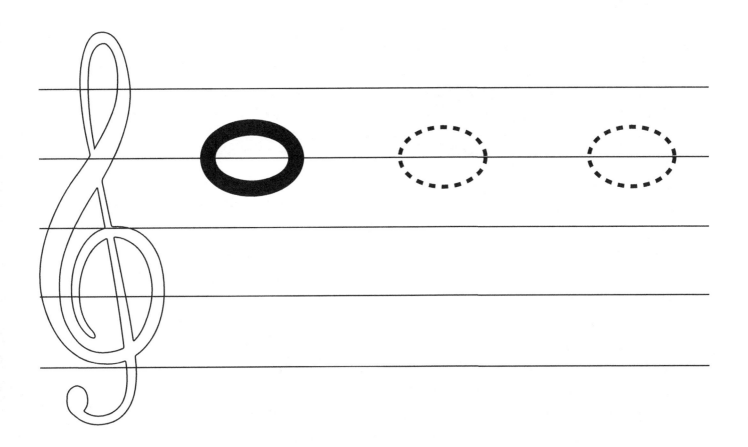

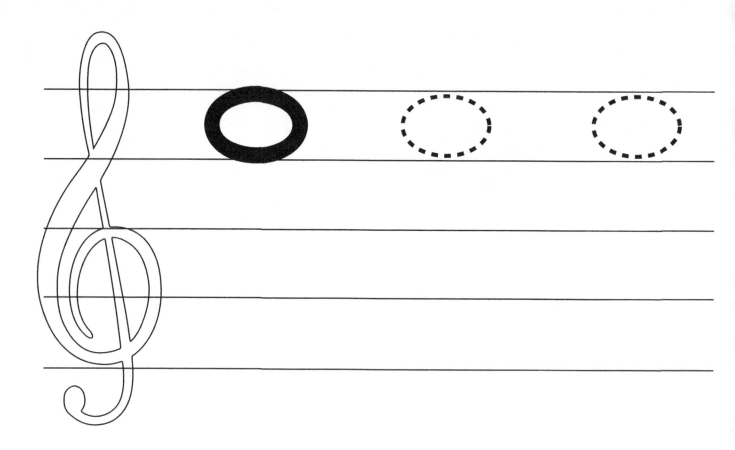

E, M E

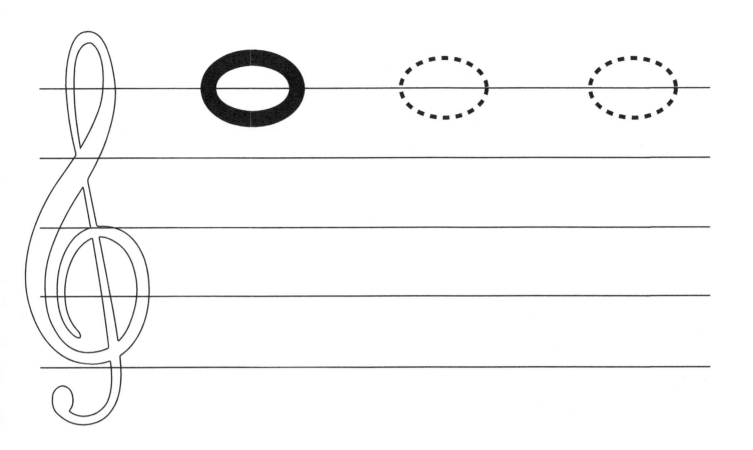

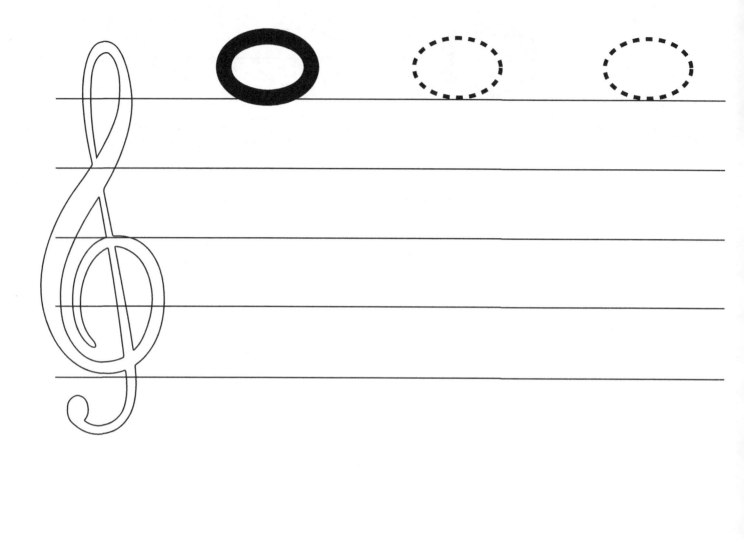

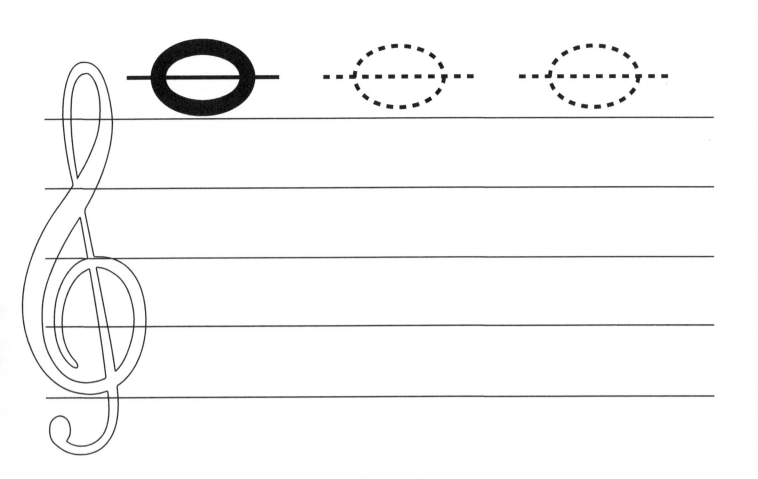

SPACE
NOTES

FACE

26

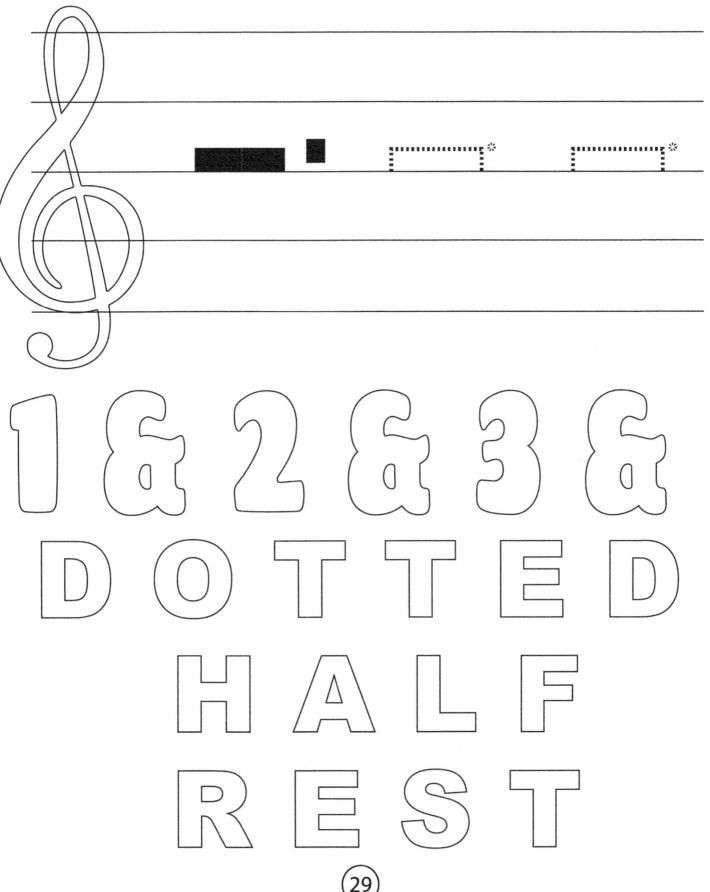

1 & 2 &

HALF REST

1
EIGHTH
REST

33

Get Math & Music Book for Kids on Amazon!

"Learn How To Count, Add, & Learn Rhythms with Fun Images"
For Ages 3+

1. Learn about the different types of rhythms and rests with fun images of pie and pizza slices to help aid with understanding
2. Learn how to count using visuals – kids can color in the fruits too!
3. Learn how to do simple additions (example 1 + 3, 1 + 9, and more!)
4. Great for teaching young children

Get BOOK #2 on BASS CLEF on Amazon!

"Essential Music Theory for Kids & Beginners"
Fun Activity Workbook Coloring Book (ages 3+)

Bass clef is used for singing, piano, keyboard, cello, bass, bass guitar, band music, marimba, bass clarinet, percussion, bassoon, trombone, tuba, timpani, euphonium, chamber music, orchestral music, & more!

Need to learn about the bass clef & how to read & write? Keep improving and build up better musical foundation by getting Book #2.

Get BOOK #3 on TREBLE CLEF on Amazon!

"Essential Music Theory for Kids & Beginners (Level 1)"
Studybook Workbook with Fun Images

Treble clef is important to know. The book covers the essentials such as scales, key signatures, solfege, scale degrees, major & minor scale intervals, whole step, half step, circle of 5ths, and more.
It will help develop musicianship of the student.

Build up a better musical foundation by getting Book #3 on Amazon.

Get BOOK #4 on BASS CLEF on Amazon!

"Essential Music Theory for Kids & Beginners (Easy Level 1)"
Studybook Workbook with Fun Images

**Bass clef is important to know. The book covers the essentials such as scales, key signatures, solfege, scale degrees, major & minor scale intervals, whole step, half step, circle of 5ths, and more.
It will help develop musicianship of the student.**

Build up a better musical foundation by getting Book #4 on Amazon.

Get Christmas Book (Melodies) TREBLE CLEF on Amazon!

"Easy Violin Christmas Songs"
31 Classic Songs on the Treble Clef
& Make Music Even More Fun with Holiday Images (Included)

Get **PIANO BOOK (Livingcolors Publishing)** on Amazon!

"Piano Book: How To Play Songs"
Learn To Create Piano Accompaniment

Do you want to be able to play from lead sheets/sheet music? This book shows the reader how to create left hand accompaniment lines in a simplified manner. Learn how to play both hands on the piano when faced with music with melody and chords but without the left hand notes!

Learn this essential skill from going through this book so that you can start playing popular and favorite tunes on the piano!

Made in the USA
Las Vegas, NV
14 July 2023